CONTENTS

WHO CARES WINS

The NHS, the SAS
and My Covid Fight!

Amanda Redgewell

DEDICATION

This book is dedicated to the amazing staff and support teams of the NHS in Somerset and at the RUH in Bath, who without any doubt saved my life. A special mention for my GP at Hope House Surgery in Radstock who acted swiftly when hearing my symptoms and played a key part in getting me the right help at the right time.

Thanks to Narinder, RUH Hospital chaplain who became my non-medical visitor and friend.

Thanks to the SBS/SAS lads for their fantastic messages of support and motivation, which were totally out of the blue.

Thanks for the help and continued support of my managers and colleagues at Dorothy House Hospice at Home.

Love and hugs to our bestest mates: Glyn, Sarah, Marcus, Holly & Hannah, Judy & Steve, Lorraine & Vince, Dawn, Liz & Will, Keith and the ACL team.

And very special thanks to Malc, Dan, Emma, Luke, Kelly, Grandson Jake, great-Grandparents Betty & John, Sally, Tony, Amy & Georgia and Jamie, Clare and Stuart for their huge support and love.

Love to you all.

CHAPTER ONE

Me

My name is Amanda and I've been married to Malc for 35 years. I have two adult children, 33-year-old Daniel and 29-year-old Emma who has recently given birth to our first amazing grandchild Jake, so long hoped for and now a beautiful and healthy 5-month-old source of total joy.

I completed training as a hospital ward nurse in 1981 and have been in and around the NHS for 38 years. I have had a variety of roles, up, down, and sideways, exploring everything that nursing can offer. After leaving the hospital ward setting, which I had decided wasn't my career path, I joined the ambulance service in Bedfordshire with a view to qualifying as a front-line ambulance person (no Paramedics back then!).

I met Malc who was on his ambulance service career path, we married and had Daniel, which ended my ambulance career much earlier than expected – 35 years and he still gets some verbal for this. We were living in Luton when Dan was born, and we both agreed this was no place to bring up our son, so Malc applied for and got a job with Wiltshire ambulance service, and we ended up living in Radstock, which is still our hometown. We started out living in a rented NHS owned property, then bought an end of terrace miner's cottage, moved out to Shoscombe Village (only a mile or two away as the crow flies) then back to our current house in Radstock. This house is about two hundred metres from the rented property one way and the same to the miner's cottage in the other direction. You could say we are totally at home in Radstock.

I started work again in the NHS, this time as a district nurse up to the birth of Emma, after which I went back to the same job, this time in a job-sharing role. We were lucky to have a great neighbour who was able to carry out childcare duties which allowed me to work and not spend all I earned on childcare. I then moved into other community-based roles.

I have worked in a range of community-based jobs in this area including with ACAD, the alcohol and drugs counselling service as a counsellor, which led onto group work with prisoners whose conviction was linked to drink or drug addiction, they then attended group counselling as either a step towards probation or to prevent being convicted again in future. I also undertook mental health assessments, arranging funding for clients who needed funding to attend drink or drug rehab, and this led me to social services and my 22-year career in adult mental health care services. During this time, I was dealing with adults who exhibited self-harming behaviours, inappropriate or violent behaviour to themselves or others and adults who required assisted living support in their own residence, either in secure communal facilities or out in the community.

It is interesting to note that I have worked with colleagues from the early days in Somerset that I still meet in different roles, some of whom also now work at Dorothy House – the health service is a small world in this respect and engender great loyalty in very many of its staff.

With changes to the service structure i.e., the outsourcing of social services care to the private sector and the big changes to working practices that this brought, I left the sector four years ago and looked for a job that would allow me to finish my working career in nursing, although I wasn't looking to retrain and regain my PIN qualification to allow me to work as a registered nurse. Whilst searching for possible jobs, a colleague brought my attention to the recruitment ads for Dorothy House Hospice – the role was with the Hospice at Home Palliative Care Team, whose role was to provide the best possible hospice care in the patient's own home, allowing these patients their final wish to die in peace at home. This is a job that I have loved and certainly makes the best use of all the skills that I have learnt over the years, and although it sounds like it would be a depressing job, it is far from it, with many positive and uplifting moments in amongst the inevitable low points. It has allowed me a perfect job role with which to end my long and varied health service career.

Hospice at home is the newest role on the roster of Dorothy House services, although the organisation has been operating for over 40 years. It is incredibly well respected and supported within the community it serves, which means that my job at the introduction stage with patients was made much easier, with an expectation of outstanding levels of care and professionalism before I'd even knocked on the door.

I work with an incredible group of people, with the team made up of professional carers from different backgrounds and with differing levels of nursing/care qualifications, which has led to the development of a well-balanced and skilled team of carers. I am employed as a carer, as I no longer have my nursing registration, but my previous work experience has stood me in good stead in this job and I have never felt out of my depth. Any questions I have had have been answered by colleagues or the support team and administrators who are always at the end of the phone with help and advice. I also work closely with the district nurses and community medics to ensure that patients get all of their needs met and have as peaceful and pain free end to their life as possible.

I have loved being able to provide hands on care, meeting some incredible patients and their families, and feel like I have been able to work with them to guide them through one of the most traumatic times in their lives. My career working with adults with all forms of disability, stress, addictions, and personal trauma have provided exactly the tools that I have relied on to carry out my job in a professional, empathetic, and supportive manner. These tools are a part of all my colleague's skills set, which becomes extremely important when each of us need peer support following a particularly traumatic or upsetting situation, either at work or in a personal capacity.

So, this is the job that I am currently employed to do and the one that I have been doing through the period that I contracted Covid-19. Having dealt with Covid-19 positive patients and their relatives during 2020, I was well versed in all aspects of correct PPE use and personal hygiene, which makes the method by which I contracted the virus even more ironic. I had been on annual leave for a week, so I know that I did not contract the virus at work. I know exactly where and when I did contract the virus and it is really devastating for our family.

Me pre-Covid

CHAPTER TWO

Ground Zero

First week of the New Year I had annual leave, and this followed the family decision not to have an all-together Christmas (as advertised by the Government). We were all relieved to have avoided contracting the virus over the previous year and were determined things would stay that way as far as possible. This was extremely hard, as it was for every disciplined person in the country. We had all four parents alive, both children and their partners and a new Grandson. And no close family meetings or baby cuddles, and the times we did see Jake we were in PPE – all these new babies growing up thinking we all look the same below our eyes!

During the last couple of days of my leave, I received a couple of calls from my step-dad Alan saying that Mum was displaying some strange symptoms, with real confusion and paranoia, feeling that she had been removed from her own house against her will (she was still at the home where they had lived together for the previous 15 years). She kept asking to be taken home and became extremely upset with her husband for not looking after her and not rescuing her from this situation. The solution was complicated by the fact that just into the New Year, the GP surgeries were not offering a full service and it was difficult to arrange a home visit.

Mum's condition deteriorated with what we assumed at the time was a gastric bug, and Alan made the unheard-of request for help, something he had rarely done in the previous two years of being Mum's carer. We called Alan by his name, as when he came into our lives me and Sal still had a strong relationship with our Dad. But make no mistake, Alan had played a huge part in our lives from the ages of 11 and 9 respectively, loved us and supported us unconditionally and we loved and respected him like a Dad.

My sister Sally had been over to clean Mum up on the Sunday, so when we got the call for help from Alan a couple of days later, we knew things were bad and that they were both at the end of the line as regards dealing with the problems at home.

My younger sister Sally and I arranged to meet at Mum's the next day, and sure enough she was in a terrible state, suffering from severe diarrhoea and vomiting (D&V), so we cleaned her up in the shower, both wearing full PPE as I do at work and did the best we could with the house, clothing etc. We basically got her ready for a GP visit in the full expectation of her being hospitalised. I was later told by a consultant in ITU that my "standard" PPE could not offer the full protection against the viral load within the flat caused by the bodily fluids present.

The decision by me and Sally to visit and help Mum and Alan was disastrous and very nearly fatal for the pair of us.

That was the day me and Sal contracted Covid-19, and looking back at the situation in the bungalow, the outcome was inevitable. We have since named the bungalow Ground Zero, as the viral load inside was extremely high. We don't know if it was Mum or Alan who was positive first but all four of us were now positive, although of course we didn't know this at the time. There were clear warnings, but these had not been flagged up by the NHS at the time – mental confusion/ mania is a sign of Covid-19 infection in geriatric patients and D&V is a sign of gastric Covid. All the signs were there but hidden due to lack of knowledge, which is extremely frustrating and again, almost fatal for me and Sal.

Back to the timeline – the visit to Ground Zero was on the Wednesday and I started feeling poorly on the Friday evening, and called work late on Friday to book off sick for my early shift the next morning. This was horrendously short notice for work, as my early shift was as part of a double-handed team required to deal with a patient needing careful handling. I knew that it would be difficult for work to cover my shift, but the symptoms were severe enough for me to consider that I was Covid positive, and a call to my sister confirmed that she was showing the same symptoms. We started to consider that we had the virus, and I booked a test for later on Saturday and was confirmed positive for Covid-19 on Sunday. I suggested that my sister get tested, and in fact her and her daughter Georgia were tested positive that weekend. Georgia had visited Ground Zero briefly on that fateful day.

Mum was hospitalised in Gloucester Royal Hospital on the Friday, showing a positive test on the Saturday. Alan felt increasingly unwell, showing signs and symptoms of a heavy cold, followed by D&V on the following Tuesday and hospitalisation on the Wednesday, also receiving a confirmation of Covid positive.

By that Wednesday Malc had also tested positive following cold like symptoms and slight breathlessness, and Sal's husband Tony too, following a precautionary test. Total disaster.

Could I just send out a message to the anti-vax/covid pandemic conspiracy theorists – please remove your heads from that very dark place and show some real respect for victims and their carers during these terrible times.

Ground Zero had taken its toll with 7 new victims.

CHAPTER THREE

My Covid Journey

For the first day or two I seemed to be coping OK, I had the cough and a temperature (although not a raging fever) and would get tight chested and breathless on exertion. I seemed to be coping. Then I was hit by overwhelming waves of nausea, vomiting and diarrhoea and realised that these were powerful symptoms of gastric Covid that had so severely affected Mum.

We are now at Tuesday morning and I am feeling very unwell and checked my SATS (blood oxygenation level measured in percentage) using our little finger device bought on Amazon, which showed a level of 92% - an expected normal reading would be 98-99%, 94% or lower is really not good if it persists at that level. I asked Malc to call 111 and when they answered I ran through my symptoms. The doctor who dealt with my call was not happy at my condition and insisted that I call 999 for an emergency ambulance. The call was made, and the ambulance arrived within 15 minutes.

When the paramedics arrived, they ran a battery of tests in their usual calm, professional manner – pulse and oxygen levels (our SATS device was confirmed as accurate), blood sugar, heart rhythm and obvious signs and symptoms. SATS were now hovering at a borderline 94% while I walked around all wired up, so the paramedics made a call to our GP to discuss my condition and they decided together that I should stay at home for now with Malc monitoring me and the GP would call back in the afternoon.

When the GP called back in the afternoon, I sounded more breathless than I had earlier and was clearly very dehydrated and more stressed. She immediately made arrangements for me to be admitted at the Bath RUH Respiratory Assessment Unit, and Malc drove me in. He found it extremely difficult to hand me over at the entrance door and not settle me onto the ward.

Being Covid positive I was taken straight to a side ward. I felt very unwell at this stage but not desperate and realised I was in the best place. I was immediately administered IV (intravenous – inside the vein) fluids which contained an anti-emetic to stop the nausea and sickness. This took about 24 hours to take effect and control the D&V. Doctor's rounds next morning saw me settled, rehydrated and much more controlled, with stable SATS, albeit still hovering around 94%. Looking at me the patient as a whole, and with the bed situation on the point of overload, the sensible decision in the circumstances was to send me home. Given the extreme circumstances surrounding bed occupancy and the necessity of avoiding the hospital staff being overwhelmed Malc and I fully supported this decision at the time.

Malc picked me up at the entrance door to the unit and we came home – for a few hours! We went to bed but I was finding it impossible to find a comfortable position for my breathing and then Malc fills in the gaps:

"Mand was very unsettled and was getting more anxious, finding it difficult to take good breaths in, and piling up pillows to try to find a comfortable position. I dozed off but woke suddenly as she got out of bed and stumbled into the en-suite, almost keeling over at the end of the bed. I took her ATS while she sat on the toilet, she was confused and very shaky. Her SATS were at an erratic 86-89%, and I had to go into ambulance mode to control a rising sense of panic. I got Mand back into bed and monitored hers SATS for 5 minutes. No improvement so I immediately dialled 999. Mand had no energy or the will to argue about this decision, that is an indication of how ill she was – she knew she had to go back into hospital. The Paramedics came in (again within 15 minutes) and provided oxygen therapy, ECG (Electro Cardio Graph – heart rhythm check), SATS, BP etc, but knew immediately they saw her that she was going into Hospital. Off she went again, I couldn't go with her, so we parted not knowing the outcome – very, very difficult".

Like the GP earlier, Malc had made the right decision at the right time – the government catchphrase that was common in the early days of the pandemic, but really sums up what must be done to get through this. It would have been much better for us all if the government had stuck to this policy more rigidly. Just my view.

I remember none of this, my first clear memory after going to bed was the A&E team trying to get a needle into one of my veins in order to infuse fluids and drugs when necessary. Due to the fact that I had again become very dehydrated, the team had great difficulty getting a needle into a vein in my arms and I stopped counting attempts at about 6 or 7 – when you become dehydrated there is much less fluid in your body, including your blood and this causes the blood vessels (veins and arteries) to squeeze closed so that the blood is kept circulating through the vital organs like your brain and heart. This means that the veins in your arms and legs are much thinner and harder to find under the skin – so lots more jabbing with a needle to find the target. It's at times like these that you need the jabber to be more like Eric Bristow than Stevie Wonder!

Bloody ouch – again and again.

The A&E doctor was coincidentally about to do a three-month stint at Dorothy House, and she quickly made the decision to get me admitted onto the Respiratory Ward. I was put into a side room on the ward and given lovely care by the nursing staff, and was started on my long oxygen therapy road, with 4-6 litres per minute normal flow from the wall mounted valve seen over all hospital beds. I was back to feeling poorly but not desperately ill and knew that I wasn't going to get away with just mild symptoms. I was almost glad to be back in hospital, and the good news was that they had finally jabbed into a vein and were putting fluids back into me that were making me feel almost human. It soon became clear, however, that my respiratory system wasn't functioning at all well on just the piped oxygen and my body was unable to maintain sufficient oxygen levels in my blood – I was struggling. This was confirmed by the number of staff that were constantly in and out to monitor me, and visits by the doctors and consultant.

One of the doctors explained that there were several drugs that they were trialling to fight the effects of Covid-19 and would I be willing to accept the use of these drugs/treatments as listed below:

Dexamethasone – type of steroid used to reduce the body's immune response that can cause inflammation in body tissues and thus interfere with normal functions.

Remdesavir – anti-virus treatment to interfere with Covid virus reproduction and slow effects of the virus.

Blood Plasma with Antibodies – removed from patients who have antibodies to Covid following infection with the virus.

To receive these drugs/treatments, and to further access trial drugs that could be used to aid recovery if I had to go on a ventilator later, I would need to sign up for the Oxford Drugs Trials – when faced with possible death the decision to trial drugs that may help is a no-brainer – give me the pen. Not flippant, totally pragmatic.

After signing this document, in the quiet moments after, it hit me like a train – oh s**t, I really am very poorly indeed.

Whilst on the Respiratory Ward I had several CT Scans (Computerised Tomography, type of detailed x-ray) and X-rays to build up a picture of what Covid was doing inside my body and how the disease was progressing. These investigations confirmed that I was suffering from the lung condition of Covid pneumonia and at this stage I did not return to the side room. A doctor explained that I now needed the next step up in oxygen therapy and the more intensive care that required removal to a high dependency/critical care environment in the hospital. It was made clear to me that because the beds in critical care were in such demand and turned around as required, they were not gender specific, so each two-bed unit was mixed male/female when necessary – the only criteria was extremely ill patient in empty bed.

Of course, I ended up in a large sealed critical care two bedded bay with a man – as it had just been explained that I was there to be monitored due to my respiratory system failing and needed to be moved through higher levels of oxygen to support it, I could not have given a toss if the Bath Rugby Team were in bed opposite me! Still, here I was, extremely vulnerable, unable to get out of bed to go to the toilet or to do anything else. So, catheter, bodily functions, treatment – all on show to a total stranger. But we were in the same s**t creek without a paddle between us (ironic when you learn more about my companion later), we had no choice but to "suck it up, princess" in the words of my old mate Paul. We settled into the life of an old married couple – what's the odd release of gas or pungent odour between friends. As the man said, when you gotta go, you gotta go.

I was subsequently put onto High-Flow Nasal Cannulation (HFNC) oxygen therapy. This was an extremely odd sensory experience; I can only compare the feeling to that of snorkelling (which I have always hated) when you have water in your mask and seem to be permanently under and swallowing water. I hated this feeling but had no option other than to come to terms with it – I was here and had to improve on this system or I would be moved onto the next stage, where I would be at the mercy of a ventilator and an even lower percentage chance of survival.

At the moment, I am deteriorating, a difficult situation to deal with.

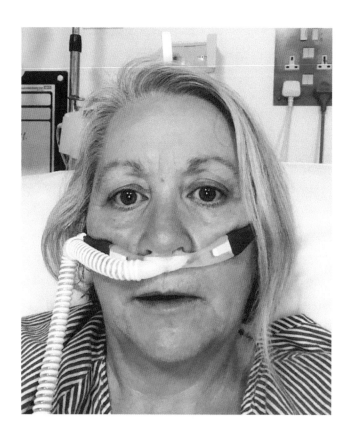

Me on HFNC

Back to the man. Andy – whose name was actually Adam, but I misheard and after being called Andy by me and the staff, he gave up correcting us and Andy it stayed. I blame it on his Australian accent (not my lousy hearing without my hearing aids). I moved this on a bit, and he became Mr. AA to me, to avoid the following:

Mand - "Hey Andy"

Adam - "Adam. It's Adam Mand".

Mand – "Sorry…Adam"

Mand – "Hey, Mr. AA….."

This man became a massively important part of my fight against the progression of the virus, in helping me to develop the mental tools to control my body and work with the oxygen therapy without panicking.

Mr. AA helped me to control my breathing to increase my SATS when the machine started to sound alarms as my oxygen levels dropped. This took a lot of physical effort, just to increase my breathing, and was incredibly uncomfortable, but he is a great motivator – I watched and helped him go through exactly the same fight. Back to Adam/Andy later.

I had started to settle in my new home and became aware of the step up in care, the amount of time that staff spent with me and how the level of PPE had moved up to another level – you've most likely all seen the video on the news of reporters in critical care units with staff looking like Dustin Hoffman and Rene Russo in Outbreak or the "bad" guys in E.T. – I wished I could phone home, but I just didn't have the breath. The staff had to be kitted up like this due to the amount of Covid virus thrown into the air in the aerosol spray caused by the high level of moisture used in the HFNC oxygen therapy. If you can imagine the moist air being forced through your nose and being drawn deep into your lungs, then when you breathe out the Covid virus caught in your lungs is "washed" out.

Every time I breathed out, I sprayed high levels of Covid virus into the room – gross! Mr. AA was guilty too.

And the staff were always there, caring and professional and suffering in silence in all that gear – amazing, amazing, amazing. True heroes, facing a lethal, unseen enemy day after day.

Then Mr. AA and I had a visit from the ITU consultant to explain our situation. As we were both in the same condition, he asked our permission to speak to us both at the same time. Due to the deterioration in our respiratory condition, it was highly likely that we would need to be intubated (a rigid tube is passed through the mouth and down into the windpipe. This is then sealed in place so that oxygen can be delivered directly to the lungs under pressure and nothing else can enter the lungs to cause a problem) and attached to a mechanical ventilator to take over the breathing function. This was the end game if we ended up there, unconscious on a machine with no control over the outcome – not an ideal situation for control freaks!

Life or death time. Really very scary.

Mr Consultant gave us the technical details – the criteria for being placed on the ventilator, the percentage chance of recovery and survival. The good news (?) was that we both had a ventilator bed available in ITU, but that this situation would be reviewed daily at 6.00 am and 6.00 pm and criteria may change based on the overall patient situation at the time.

Having watched the news over the previous year, I had seen how poorly people were who went onto the ventilator, and how survival at this stage was much reduced. I told the Consultant that I didn't want to go on a ventilator – in the words of Julia Robert's Pretty Woman, "Big mistake. Huge!"

Consultant (C) – "Are you saying you don't want to be placed on a ventilator, are you refusing this treatment".

Me – "That's right, I don't want to go on it".

C – "To be clear, you don't want to go on the ventilator if it becomes necessary, you are prepared to die?"

Me – "Sorry, what?"

C – "I need you to be very clear Amanda, as we may not be able to ask you this again – do you want to live?

Me – "Of course I do"

C – "In that case I need you to understand that if I need you to be ventilated, it is because I think this is your best chance for survival, NOT because I think you will die. So, do you agree to let me decide on the best course of action for your survival. You need to be clear now".

Me – "Of course I want to live; I am completely in your hands. You must do what's best for me."

C – "Thank you Amanda – but we are not there yet, so keep fighting."

My attitude here may seem really foolish, and I certainly thought so as I lay there after the talk. Mr. AA said we needed to do whatever it took to survive. But I was simply scared of the ventilator and did not think I would do very well on it – I did not think I would survive.

The discussion with the consultant was carried out in the same calm, professional and caring manner displayed by ALL of the staff ALL of the time. No ifs, buts or maybes, 100% dedication – this cannot be emphasised enough, I was totally cared for. While we were at our lowest ebb and totally vulnerable, the staff become our family and we felt they treated us in this way too. The totally gruelling 12 hour shifts that the staff work give the patients a great continuity of care. I knew that the morning shift started at 8.00 am and the same staff would be with me until 8.00 pm, then just that one change of staff who were with us until the next morning.

CHAPTER FOUR

Covid Effects

I had been in the critical care unit for several days and nights when I experienced an overwhelming sense of loss of power in all of my limbs. This caused me to panic to such an extent that it was obvious to the staff, who quickly gathered around the bed to try to find out what was happening. They were asking me questions, but I was not responding clearly, and they were shuffling around the bed trying to work out what was going on with my limbs. With no communication taking place and a bit of a flap going on, me being panicked and vocal but making no sense, the doctor took control by shushing everyone else and making the classic zip-it motion across his lips at me. I got what he meant straight away, as it is an in joke between my best friend Sarah and me when she tells me off for answering back (when I don't need to) by making the sign and saying, "zip it, Shrimpy". Calm restored, they could work out what was going on. I had noticed that my hands and feet had ballooned in size (seemed almost double in size) like Eddie Murphy in the Nutty Professor, a really strange and unnerving effect together with the loss of power.

The staff team were using me as a human dartboard again, this time using pinpricks to gauge the loss of feeling in my limbs, and it became evident really quickly that my right side had regained its senses very quickly (step away from the needle, nurse friend) but the effect on my left side remained. The neurology guys arrived and did further pricks and reflex tests and also did some tests on my cranial nerves which indicated the notable loss of function in my left arm and leg. They were not absolutely sure of the cause, but the two likely options were a mild CVA (cerebro-vascular accident – stroke) or Covid clot related nerve damage. They explained that they could not look to treat the causes/effects of the loss of power at this stage as they couldn't interfere with the treatment for Covid pneumonia, this being the priority life threatening issue that had to be dealt with first. However, they had to take the view that the cause of this loss of power was due to a stroke and therefore I was put onto a high dose of anti-coagulants (blood thinners) to limit the chances of more clots forming and doing further damage. They continued to monitor me and test my reflexes and pain stimulus response with needles – hey doc, one hundred and eighteeeeeeeey!!

The feeling returned to my left limbs over the next couple of days, but still no power – and the ring and middle fingers of my left hand were totally dead and unmoving and starting to curve in towards my palm. This meant constant stretching and exercising of this hand by me and the staff to prevent me losing the use of these two fingers. They also made use of splinting to the fingers and I used a ball to keep squeezing. I was totally restricted in what I could do in the way of general physio on the limbs as I became breathless and my SATS dropped at the slightest exertion.

It is usual in cases of suspected stroke or clots to have a CT scan, but I could not lay flat long enough to have a scan as again, I would become totally breathless – there was no way I could maintain my oxygen levels for 40 minutes. This meant that when I did have a scan several days later it was inconclusive, albeit there was no major damage visible. Even after this period of time and feeling a whole lot better, it was a real struggle to maintain my oxygen levels without piped oxygen – I just about managed it.

I was still bedridden and unable to get up, so I couldn't check my ability to stand up and support myself or walk. I did have physio's come in and move my arm and leg for me in a controlled way, to avoid me losing too much muscle tone and improving my chances of full recovery. In between their visits I made great efforts to try to exercise my arm and leg as much as I could, and power did return very slowly, but I still had a very clumsy arm and leg.

The day before I was moved out of the critical care area down to a less intense but still Covid secure area, my Mr. AA became extremely poorly and had to be moved into ITU for extra support although thankfully he never had to go onto the ventilator. I was devastated. I was alone that night for the first time and without my super coach, and I felt really low. The staff instinctively realised how much of a loss this was to my recovery and did their level best to replace him and his positive vibe.

Mr. AA – younger than me, well built, a very fit Aussie who was a rowing coach (very useful up s**ts creek without a paddle), whose coaching skills were put to use on me and made all the difference. Without a shadow of a doubt he helped me to pull through. His calmness under pressure (he also practised yoga) passed on to me and helped me learn how to control my breathing to raise my oxygen levels and stop the monitor alarms going off, and also how to deal with the horrendous drowning feeling. It felt like he was irreplaceable when he was wheeled out, and of course I couldn't help feeling that his chances of recovery were slipping away.

The other "torture" that had to be inflicted by the staff was the monitoring of blood gasses, and this meant taking a sample of your arterial blood. Usually when you have blood taken it is from the veins that are close to the surface of your skin and are easily (usually in a well person) seen and/or felt. The arteries lay deeper under the surface (although can be felt at pulse points in the body) to afford them more protection, so they are harder to find. They must be used as they deliver the freshly oxygenated blood around the body, whereas the veins take the oxygen depleted blood back to the heart for "re-gassing". So where to find a suitable artery?

To find an artery in the wrist or arm – as they do with veins – would be very difficult and extremely painful. When Malc was in ITU following an accident 27 years ago, I watched a junior doctor spend twenty minutes trying to take arterial blood via his groin – it made my eyes water. So, for me, a new and even more diabolical torture known as arterialised ear lobe blood gas was employed, which is a relatively new procedure used in critical care scenarios. The procedure requires a small incision being made in your ear lobe (no pain relief) and the insertion of a fine plastic tube into an artery and the removal of a blood sample. This is then run down to a blood gas analyser situated on the ward and the results checked in real time.

The process started with Mr. AA helping me along with words of encouragement, and after a very unpleasant few minutes, the fully kitted staff took the vial of blood to the unit door and passed it over to the normally PPE'd staff who took it to the analyser for checking. Phew, that was done. Or was it?

After seeing my nurse at the door become visibly upset during her discussion with the ward nurse, she had to explain to me that the gas analyser could not be calibrated and due to the time lag, the blood sample could not be used again to be checked. My nurse was very upset having to explain this to me, so there was no reason or point in getting upset – it would have to be taken again later from my wrist.

Throughout this unmissable experience, Mr. AA kept up the verbal support and calm encouragement, always ignoring his own respiratory distress to help me along. I cannot thank you enough mate.

So anyway, the selfish git left me alone (too soon?) and the nursing staff rallied around to try to lift my spirits and to keep me as positive as they could. I got the full weight of their encouragement and care, this support also coming from an unexpected source. We had been told in the previous days that the Army had been asked to help within the hospital in several logistical roles, like patient welfare, restocking, portering etc. on the normal wards and we could see them going backwards and forwards, easily identified as they were in operational uniform. My nurse came in to say that they had a soldier seconded to them for the night and would I be happy for him to sit with me through the night to help replace Mr. AA.

The young soldier was fully kitted up in ITU PPE and sat next to my bed during the night. It was lovely to have someone there, and although I couldn't communicate very well through my difficulty in breathing, he quietly talked about what he did as a soldier based in Plymouth and how as a young man, he was shocked by what he had seen of the effects of Covid-19 on the population, only really seeing what was happening since being seconded to the hospital. It is the same with any situation like we are in, self-preservation won't always allow us to see what's happening until it affects us personally.

I did drift off to sleep several times and it was a shock to wake up and see a soldier in full uniform sat next to me, and it would take a few minutes each time for me to remember where I was and realise, I was safe and secure with my own guardsman. I really appreciated him being there, it was a lovely thing for him to do and for my nurses to arrange.

I was holding my own now, continuing to improve, having learned how to work with the HFNC and control my breathing to get the best results. I had finally turned that often-mentioned corner, as beloved by old Boris, and it was time to move out of the critical care area and down onto a less intense ward environment. I was moved by more soldiers – I would say a military escort – and ended up in a different sealed bay (due to the aerosol spray still being emitted from me on the infernal HFNC) that was necessary to protect me and the nursing staff. I was also seen off by lots of the brilliant staff who were on duty including members of the oxygen therapy outreach team and it was a really emotional time – so much love and care had been directed towards me and had helped me through this horrific time.

So, my two burly "drivers" got me safely to my new home and the staff who accompanied me down to monitor and transfer equipment, explained that the nursing involvement would be less now, but this was a good thing as it showed how much I was improving. I was sharing the new bay with a female nurse who had become very ill, but we were now on the road to recovery.

I began eating and drinking properly and seemed to being improving steadily, most importantly in my head, moving further and further away from the damned ventilator and closer to getting fitter and going home.

I never felt abandoned on this ward, the staff were always available and attentive and were working with us to make sure we were eating and getting healthier and ready for home.

The huge bonus was that I was now by a window and could see outside for the first time in 3 weeks – woohoo! What a joy to see life outside, I could almost feel myself moving out there and back to life. I had the window slightly open, so great to feel fresh air wash over me and to watch as we got a tiny fall of snow. I now needed to focus on getting rid of the catheter and taking full control of all my functions to properly begin my rehab. The staff still played a huge part (still in full PPE) helping me in and out of bed and always quick to arrive when the bell was rung. Bear in mind that when the staff came in to see us, they had to don all of their PPE, even to bring in a jug of water, and then remove it when leaving, to properly isolate us. Can you imagine that faff as part of your daily routine, as if it weren't difficult enough already.

I was still getting stronger with each meal – which were all good, tasty, and nourishing, totally opposite to public opinion – and I was devouring every speck on each plate that was put in front of me. I would even ask for a naughty midnight toast snack, and somebody was always there to sort it for me.

On a really sad note, the person I shared the room with was a nurse who had contracted Covid at work and had become seriously ill like me but appeared to be recovering. We couldn't communicate very well as we were both hampered by the HFNC tubing, but would give each other the thumbs up, and when I was able to move about could at least get eye contact with her to help in our mutual support. Her house mate and closest friend however, another nurse, had to be placed on a ventilator which meant that, due to lack of beds in Bath, had to be transferred to Plymouth. I do not know the outcome for either of these patients unfortunately. They are statistics on the news, but to me real people with their own stories to tell. I hope that they will both be able to tell their own survival stories to their friends and families.

As is the case with most longer-term patients, I became very institutionalised in that my mental clock worked by shift changes, lights on and off, mealtimes, drinks and drug rounds, cleaning rotas etc. It is quite easy to see how older people come to rely on these routines when they are confined for long periods. Changes to the routine can become very upsetting and unsettling, and we need to be very aware of this with our parents, grandparents, and friends.

It came to what I thought was going to be my release day, but unfortunately the neuro team were unable to see me due to work pressures, so I had to stay another night. I was slightly disappointed, but I was able to deal with this very calmly – in the current situation, everybody trying to help me was working flat out, and they certainly didn't want one of their precious beds unnecessarily occupied for any longer than was absolutely necessary.

The next day the neuro team explained how they were learning so much all the time regarding Covid effects on the human body but had a long way to go. They couldn't give me a definite diagnosis on my left sided weakness but would follow me up on an ongoing basis, to learn as much as possible and help wherever they could.

And so, I was discharged with strict orders to rest, eat well to put back on the weight that I had lost – I really do not recommend the Covid-19 diet, it sucks – and be careful with any form of physio, slow and gentle, no stress.

Malc phoned to say he was at the front door of the hospital and I was delivered to him by two nurses, and after an emotional cuddle with him and thanks and farewell to the staff, he drove me home.

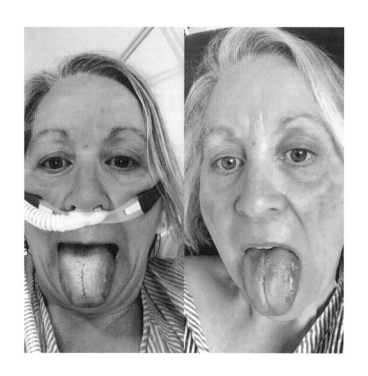

Covid tongue – really!

CHAPTER FIVE

While I was in – Mum, Alan, and the Family

Me, Mum and Sally

Mum - Pamela Mary Davis

Mum was born into a large, poor London East End family in 1936, a proper cockney. She didn't start school until she was 12, as she reminded us throughout her life, due to being hospitalised for much of this time due to serious medical problems with her lower legs, which at that time required the fitting of "boot'n'irons" to try to help correct the deformity. These were horrible, heavy boots and iron callipers used to help fix the bones and try to correct the leg development. She'd also contracted TB during this time. But Mum was a fighter right from the start and these were just two serious conditions that she had to fight to overcome throughout her life. They sure made them tough, the old World War Two generation. She had serious heart problems (unstable angina), replacement joints in a shoulder, both hips and a knee, peritonitis, sepsis twice and then lung cancer 5 years ago. This final blow was really the straw that broke the camel's back, and her health was really in decline. Alan really was the lifeline for these last 5 years – see below. To add to her problems, in the last couple of years she became diabetic and had real problems with blood flow in one of her legs, leading to discomfort, pain and discolouration.

Mum did as much as she could – being very private she would not let Al bathe her, and she had to rely on Sally and me to help with this over the last couple of years.

While she was relatively fit, she loved to go away on holidays with Alan around the world, and loved to visit, seemingly anyone, anywhere. I'm sure Malc thought she had gipsy blood when he met her, she could never stay still in one place for long, and this included homes. We moved lots of times when me and Sal were young, and I seemed to change school every year as a child. This led to a rather unsettled and chaotic time growing up, until Alan arrived on the scene following Mum's break up with my Dad and her first husband Jim. I was 10 years old at this time.

Mum and Alan

Frederick Alan Davis - always known as Alan.

Mum and Al met when Sally and I were 8 and 10 respectively and married when we were 9 and 11. This was the second marriage for both of them, and from the start it was a passionate and loving relationship. At the time that Alan met Mum, life was very chaotic and full of uncertainty. When Alan came into Mum and our lives, that all changed, and he brought a strong feeling of safety and stability to our lives and this continued through to the present day.

I had a difficult time as a teenager and rebelled against Alan, but he never faltered in his support for me, always providing that loving and stable presence. When I look back, I realise that Alan has featured in my life for longer than my Dad, who sadly died at the age of 56 when I was 23 – he had a short and desperate fight against pancreatic cancer. He was a great Dad too, and I have very much missed him not being there to see how his Grandchildren developed and to meet his Great Grandchildren. I was incredibly lucky to have Alan to provide the love and support I needed when Dad wasn't there, early on following Mum and Dad's separation and divorce, and of course after Dad died.

There was never any conflict in my relationships with Dad and Alan, in that Alan never replaced Dad, they were both there for me. Alan always provided every opportunity for us and was steadfast and calm in most situations. He fell into the role of Grandad with total commitment, always enjoying being around our children and in the case of Sally's kids, the Great Grandchildren too. He was always ready with a Dad joke or three and loved a laugh, never too serious. Mum and Al regularly took our kids and Sal's on camping and caravan holidays and they have always had a strong relationship with the kids, bolstered by their young at heart outlook. Al particularly looked much younger than his 75 years, looking nearer 60, maintaining his fitness and staying fit and upright, loving to play golf and be off and away on holidays around the world.

This freedom to get out and about was curtailed 5 years ago, when Mum developed cancer in her lung (more on Mum later) and had to have a part of it removed in a serious operation followed by a stay in ITU. From this time on, Alan very much took the role of carer and did everything for Mum. This involved general care and running the household, being driver of car and wheelchair when necessary. So, the golfing, holidays and lots of the fun stuff pretty much stopped.

Alan hanging off the side in his younger days

Racing as a Veteran

CHAPTER SIX

Mum, Alan, and Sally Covid

Back to Ground Zero. Mum had been taken into hospital following the disaster at the bungalow and had been found to be Covid positive. Me and Sally returned home and were tested positive over the weekend, with me in and out and back into hospital the following Tuesday, Wednesday, Thursday, and my long stay for the next few weeks.

Alan, meanwhile, was having real issues at home, with D&V like Mum, but had only mentioned this in passing and hadn't said how bad it was to the rest of the family. Instead, he spoke to a close family friend and said that he was going to stay at home and fight it by himself. Luckily, Carol was an old friend of mine from nursing days and recognised that Alan was seriously ill, and knowing Mum's diagnosis, was almost definitely Covid positive. She persuaded him that if the worst happened, one of the family would end up finding him dead at home which would have been horrific.

He called an ambulance on Friday morning and was hospitalised in the Gloucester Royal, but in a different ward to Mum. He was tested positive for Covid-19.

I had a video call with Sally on the Sunday and realised immediately that she was also very unwell. She was extremely pale and distressed and told me that her SATS were 89%!! I contacted Malc, who phoned her and after a short discussion arranged for her daughter Amy to phone 999 on her behalf. She was hospitalised in the Gloucester Royal too, again on a different ward to Mum and Al.

Our only way of communicating with each other this stage was by phone and video call. None of the four of us in hospital could be visited.

Alan spent the next few days relatively peaceful in hospital, and had calls with various members of the family, although he was tired and very weak, and on basic oxygen therapy. He refused any invasive oxygen therapy or mask as he was very claustrophobic. He tried to communicate with Mum, but she was very confused and unable to understand what was going on.

The following Wednesday evening we were told that Alan's condition was deteriorating, a situation exacerbated by his underlying COPD (Chronic

Obstructive Pulmonary Disease) and that the family should call to make their final goodbyes. My nurse made phone contact with Alan's ward and his nurse. So, our final goodbye messages were passed like Chinese whispers, from me to nurse, then nurse to Alan and back. All four of us were in tears. The rest of the family did the same and my son Daniel was asked by Alan to promise that his ashes would be taken to the Isle of Man and scattered at a place on the TT course called The Bungalow, close to Joey Dunlop's statue. Alan and Pam had holidayed on the Isle of Man regularly for the last 40 years and normally around the TT Races. Alan was a massive fan and had been a competitive grass track racer in his younger days – Joey Dunlop was a real hero to him. Of course, Dan promised, and it will happen, together with a Memorial Bench at the site.

Alan sadly passed away at 01.15 am on 21st January 2021.

The staff looking after Mum tried to explain what had happened to Alan, but she was so confused at this stage that she couldn't fully understand what was happening. Unfortunately, she was terribly upset that no one had visited her and that she had been left alone, and she really could not be made to understand what the real situation was, much of this due to the Covid delirium. This meant that any calls from the family to Pam were met with confusion and distress, and this left everybody feeling useless in being unable help and very upset.

Toughing it out all the way, she kept refusing any form of oxygen and given that she was pretty much functioning on one lung, it was remarkable that she kept going. Like Alan she had underlying COPD and the poor leg circulation caused by the diabetes was leading to concern about blood clots forming here.

I had a final call with Mum, and told her to relax and be calm, it was OK to let go and to go and join Alan. I was also trying to explain to her through her confusion that she did not have dementia – something she was terrified of developing – and that it was Covid that was causing the confusion.

This call was awful for both of us, and we ended in tears and unable to talk further. I did manage to talk with Mum's nurse the next day and managed to have a professional discussion about Mum's care and used my own knowledge of end-of-life care to work out the best way forward in easing Mum's distress and what drugs would help. It was a great comfort to know that a caring professional was looking after Mum in much the same way as I'd been involved in caring for patients in their final hours. The huge irony for me was that I had been with so many dying patients over the years, caring for them and their families, but couldn't do the same for either of my own parents. This is something that I will need to deal with in the future, as soon as we can all get back to some form of normality.

The nurse kindly called me back an hour later to let me know that Mum had passed away quietly and with no distress, the day after Alan, at 16.45 pm on 22nd January 2021.

Neither Sally nor I, nor the rest of the family, could grieve properly as we were still fighting our own Covid battles or supporting each other through this period. All of our children played a huge part in us getting through this time, but it has taken a lot out of them. My Dan and Emma and Sally's girls Amy and Georgia, all played their part in different ways, staying in contact with each other, supporting each other as well as me and Sal. Georgia, as the only Grandchild to have been Covid positive and who lives with Sal a short drive from Ground Zero, took on a lot of responsibility for searching the bungalow for documentation and valuables etc. and organised the paperwork and sent it over to Malc who was Executor for the Wills. She was backwards and forwards over many days and we are all super grateful to her for doing this – I cannot explain how awful it must have been for her to visit the bungalow in the state it was in and deal with such personal items.

Sally spent a few weeks in hospital, being discharged a few days after me. She didn't end up on the HFNC or ventilator but got through on high level oxygen on normal supply. She seems to be very breathless still, but we all need time to recover.

The fight goes on.

CHAPTER SEVEN

The SBS/SAS Boys

As a family we have watched the SAS: Who Dares Wins programmes over the years and have been to see Ant Middleton on his first theatre "Talk" tour, with some of his inspirational methods of dealing with stress becoming particularly useful to me at my worst points.

We all watched it for different reasons, Malc has always been interested in the military and Special Forces (books and bloody war films), Dan was a big fitness geek before his serious road cycle accident, competing in assault course runs, road and off-road cycling and kick boxing, yoga etc.

For me and Emma it was just watching Ant and Foxy be alpha males and kick ass! Malc had updated us on Billy's career, an amazing life of service and adventure and great danger, and he may seem to be rough and ready and a bit older, but what a man.

I had the period of three days after I was put onto HFNC when I really struggled with my breathing and was fighting against the whole process and was panicky when my respiratory rate dropped – I was just incredibly low.

I thought of myself as a tough cookie, in that I would always take problems head on, whether that be recovering from a difficult caesarean or dealing with the aftermath of both Malc and Dan's serious accidents. But I could not get a handle on this fight and seemed to be an emotional wreck. Looking back now, I can understand how the position I was in was unreal, no close support from my family who couldn't visit and a lonely fight against this ruthless virus. I did of course have Mr. AA and the wonderful staff, but not my nearest and dearest – it is different. Me and Malc have been together for 35 years and have been through some real lows, but we have dealt with these crises together, which made it even more difficult now I felt by myself. Even the short telephone and video comms were difficult, made tricky by the oxygen tubes, breathing difficulty and general ward noise. So, I ended up inside my own head, dealing with my fears, the machines and just breathing. And my head was throwing up huge fears and silly thoughts, from not being there to watch my first Grandchild growing up to not having learnt how to use the oven in my newly fitted kitchen.

The nurses were doing their best to try to improve my state of mind by putting up pictures of my family and Grandson, and Emma was sending me pics and videos of what Jake was getting up to, but this was having the opposite effect. The more I saw and thought about my family, the more upset I became, and I continued on the emotional roller coaster.

I really had to try to get a grip on my state of mind. I had been lucky as an adult in not suffering from anxiety and being able to deal with emotional issues at the time and not hold them in – me and Malc had many tough, deep conversations over the years working through our own problems, and these would be positive ways to get through to a better place. I did have particularly good friends that had to deal with life affecting anxieties and I had offered them counsel through difficult times. I had been able to help and listen to their problems and issues while still being distanced from them as I had never suffered from their levels of anxiety. Now I was right there and needed to get a grip on my mental state to have a chance of beating this virus.

Next thing I knew, I was roused by the staff, who were sitting me up and saying that there was something I had to see that had been arranged by Emma and Dan. They were getting my phone set up and preparing me for something and I didn't have a clue what was going on. They set the recording going and I couldn't believe I was watching Ant Middleton who had recorded a personal message to me in his own home and was telling me to stay strong and keep fighting this thing and to not stay in the fear bubble too long. I had to fight this to get back to my family and Jake.

I know what you are saying – what's a fear bubble? When we went to see Ant do his live talk, he talked about his time in Afghanistan fighting the Taliban with the SBS and how he dealt with being away from his family and in combat.

Firstly, he would have no communication with his family either written or video – to try to continue his home life by bringing it to war would be distracting and take his focus away from the job at hand. Any distraction from purpose could be fatal for him or his colleagues. The penny dropped for me, I had to remove the reminders of home from the room, be totally selfish and focus 100% on dealing with what was in front of me.

Secondly, he developed a way of dealing with fear to lessen its effect while not denying it was there. He created the fear bubble – he would stay outside the fear bubble until he was at the point of danger, enter the fear bubble for the minimum time possible when facing actual danger, then retreating from the bubble when danger was past. Instead of staying in a continual state of fear and heightened tension, the fear was broken up into smaller periods that could be more readily dealt with.

This was what I needed to do now, how I needed to approach what I was going through. I had to stop thinking ahead to what I would miss out on and deal with the here and now and control my fear levels as much as possible. I also contacted Malc and the rest of the family, letting them know that I would not be in contact for a couple of days until I had got myself sorted out. It would be nine days until I looked at photos and video of little Jake again – if I slipped and started to think about him and the future during this time, I quickly became quite emotional.

So, I watched the video several times and became quite a celebrity by association and various staff asked to see the video, including some of the military guys who were working on the ward. My phone also got passed around the ward for everyone else to see.

Over the next couple of days, I also had a personal text message from Foxy and a couple of video messages from Billy, the second from his garden with his bulldog and his own Jake, his son. I am so grateful these guys took time to contact me like this, and what a huge boost to my morale. Love and respect to you guys.

I used all of this advice and positive energy to apply myself to working with the HFNC and alongside Mr. AA's coaching. I had reached a turning point, I began to improve and keep my blood oxygen levels up, so that the Ventilator was taken off the "likely to happen" list. Everything had come together to ensure that I was moving towards a successful outcome.

I am hoping to be able to catch up with Foxy and Billy next year when they tour again, and to be able to tell them what a difference their input made to my recovery.

TROOPER A: SPECIAL BOAT SERVICE VETERAN

"Listen now – you stay positive, keep fighting and remain in that bubble 'til the job is done, and get out of there and get back to see your baby Jake. 'Til then, stay focused, stay switched on and fucking battle and beat this virus. You've got this. Much love and huge amounts of positivity from me to you"

A. M. X.

TROOPER F: SPECIAL BOAT SERVICE VETERAN

"Hi Dan, thanks for the message, kind of you to let me know. Please let your Mum know I'm thinking of her and wishing her well. Tell her to stay in the fight no matter what. Anyway, take care mate".

F.

TROOPER B: SPECIAL AIR SERVICE VETERAN

"This is for Mum 'cause you didn't tell me her name. I know you're fighting covid, just kick covid in the ass. You're strong, you're positive, fight it, nut it, knock it down and move on. Get out of there, you've got little Jake to look forward to. That's my little Jake over there, he's not so little any more and Alfie (Bulldog) sends his regards as well. So get well, fight on, everybody loves you, all good reasons to fight. Always a little further"

M. "B." B.

CHAPTER EIGHT

Two Guardian Angles

Narinder

When I was first hospitalised and on early-stage oxygen therapy at normal flow rates, I was resting in bed when a member of staff approached the bed. I realised very quickly that this was a hospital chaplain Narinder wearing the usual collar and crucifix, as she approached with a lovely smile and a soft, calming speaking voice. I must admit the thought quickly passed through my mind:

"Dear God, how ill am I if they've sent a vicar to help me out!"

She explained that she visited all the wards to offer religious and human support to patients and to offer prayers for them if they were happy for this to happen. I explained that I wasn't a church going Christian although I tried to live by Christian principles and would feel a fraud if I asked her to pray for me. She explained that being a non-Christian did not exclude a person from being prayed for and she would be happy to do this. I did ask that she say a prayer for Mum and Alan who were still alive at this time.

I also told her about close friends in Lincolnshire who are lay preachers and had already organised a prayer circle for us and were keeping us in their thoughts – I felt pretty well covered on this side of things. I also made her laugh when I told her about friends who I knew were definitely Christians because they attended church every Christmas.

She then said she would pop in to see me a couple of days later around the Sunday services to see how I was, however, I deteriorated very quickly and ended up in the critical care unit before this visit could take place. I did come round at one point over the next couple of days to see Narinder knocking on the window that separated the unit from the main ward and giving me that lovely smile and thumbs up – this was unfortunately the nearest she could get at this stage due to the risk of contamination to her, but I was so chuffed that she had taken the time out to find me and give me some positive energy.

I saw Narinder once more, through a window again, this time on my final couple of days in hospital on the last ward. Her lovely face appeared at the window and one of the nurses came in to say would it be OK for her to visit with me. I really appreciated the thought and that she had taken time out to track me down again, but I was acutely aware of the risk that this would be to her and asked the nurse to thank her for me but say that I did not want her to take this risk. She gave me a thumbs up and blew me a kiss, I returned the kiss, and this was the last time I saw her. Unfortunately, I didn't get to tell her face to face how much her visits and positive presence had meant to me.

Mr. AA

I entered the critical care unit knowing I was sharing with a man and there he was, 6'2" of fit, strapping Aussie rowing coach and yoga guru. For a start, surely he shouldn't be a candidate for this level of illness? I could not believe that someone so physically fit could be hit this hard. From the moment I arrived in what was his space up to then, he welcomed me in. We would speak when breathing allowed and made lots of gestures. He ate like a machine, clearing anything put in front of him, whereas I just could not overcome the physical issues of swallowing whilst on the HFNC. He was like a dustbin, his training making him understand the need for energy at any cost to have the strength to fight. He would even finish anything I left, and that was quite a bit.

So, you know how he got the Mr. AA moniker, after I'd convinced all of the staff and even Adam that his name was Andy. He just gave up fighting that battle.

He was a definite alpha male, a few of whom exist in our friends' group and I find reassurance in their company. Interestingly I wouldn't describe Malc as an alpha, but he is strong and supportive in all the ways I need, and it makes it easy for me to organise his Dadmin jobs.

Mr. AA gave me lots of reassurance and support, even at the cost of his own precious energy to fight the virus, he really made a massive difference to me getting through. Of all the skills you'd want in a roommate in this situation it is coaching skills, and he calmed me when necessary and talked me through breathing, drinking, ear lobe cutting etc.

One thing we both experienced was the drop and it was obvious when it happened to the other person. I would describe the sensation like when you miss a stair on the way down or step off a kerb that is higher than expected, that weird sensation in the pit of your stomach. Now times that by a hundred. It's like your body knows you are sleeping too deep, and respirations are slowing, and you need to be jolted awake. I'd hear him gasp and he'd explain about the drop and then I experienced my own first drop and he again reassured me that it's what I had seen him go through, and I took this on, and the feelings lessened and had completely stopped by the time I got onto the last ward.

A side effect of the HFNC system could be caused when the fluid used to provide the vapour in the system ran out, and it would feel like you had hot smoke in your nose alongside a horrible burning smell. This had happened to Andy, and he was now like a hawk watching his own fluid bags to make sure the levels did not drop too far and forewarning the nurses of the need to change them . He immediately took on this responsibility for my fluids too, ensuring that I did not have to go through this horrible sensation. He had totally got on top of what he needed to do to have the best chance to survive this and he applied the same approach to helping me without a second thought.

The great news is that Mr. AA pulled through, and in fact was discharged from hospital a couple of days before me. We have messaged since, and like me the road to full recovery will be long and slow.

As the SAS boys say, always a little further.

CHAPTER NINE

Covid Dreams

This was a very strange side effect of the whole experience and occurred during my three-day low point in critical care when my physical and mental fatigue had reached rock bottom. I was just trying to cope with the hour to hour rise and fall of emotions, just trying to deal with the problems involved in the previously simple act of breathing and all of the medical activity going on around me. All of this was exacerbated by the lack of sleep brought on by a genuine fear of falling asleep and not being able to breathe, of stopping breathing altogether.

All these external effects led to me ending up in a mostly dream like state, with little awareness of what was going on around me unless purposely stimulated by the staff or Mr. AA, and the passing of time became unreal, with minutes sometimes seeming like hours and vice versa.

In my role as an end-of-life nurse I had seen so many patients start to transition (move from life to death) and become disassociated with their surroundings, going deeper and deeper into a sleep like state, losing the ability to interact with those around them and unable to verbalise their feelings. They gradually move from life to death, slowly transitioning, until they pass. There has always been speculation about what happens at this point, and some who return from near death experiences talk of tunnels and light and previously deceased family or friends beckoning to them, but I did not experience any of this. No dark abyss, or Mum and Al calling to me, or even the feeling that I was waiting to die. I just felt this drifting away from the moment and all that was going on around me.

Luckily for me, the dreams that I recall were in no way unpleasant or dark or frightening. I had read about people who suffered from Covid nightmares, and in one particular case, a poor lady who dreamt that her son had been murdered. Even the pleasant dreams I had were lucid enough to have actually happened, so she must have been in a terrible state.

The thoughts and dreams were quite random but strangely enough, seemed to put my life in order. The images were a mix of episodes and characters in my life that had happened, but others I could not be sure if they had occurred or were made up in my imagination.

One series of images I remember come from the time we spent as a family with great friends at their home outside of Rome (John was a senior flight engineer with British Airways and Helen was a nurse and ex-paramedic friend of Malc). I remember the kids all playing together on a trampoline and splashing about in the swimming pool. This brings me to a little character called Tommy, an African Grey parrot who lived with John and Helen – and he was very real. He lived his best life in Rome, having free reign of the house and garden and was often spotted sat in the olive tree in the garden – he'd had his flight feathers clipped so he didn't fly off and get lost, which meant that he would climb the tree using his beak and claws, then just jump out to get down – hilarious to watch.

Tommy's main claim to fame though was his vocal repertoire – noises, names, tone of voice – he was a great mimic. He was so good that John would often run to answer the phone, only to find out it was Tommy doing his brrring brrring phone sound. He often called out John and Helen's kids names – Georgina and Joshua – having heard these names repeated most regularly for a variety of reasons. So, the names would be called out in a variety of tones – calling out, annoyance, anger, cheerful – depending on how he felt. We were all fascinated by this little bird and would wake to his cheerful vocalisations every morning of our stay. He had stayed with several people prior to John and Helen, so had some Italian phrases, most recognisable being "ciao" and a hysterical mimicking of a smoker's cough learnt from one unfortunate owner.

"Cough, cough, cough, Joshua, brrring, brrring, Georgina"

"Morning Tommy"

But, crucially, he was a very polite parrot and never swore at all. This was great news for John and Helen, as the kids attended the local English school and would be visited by other parents and the school vicar.

Enter the Redgie's. At the time of our visit the popular TV comedy show The Royal Family was current and the favourite catchphrase "arse" had entered popular vocabulary. So, one morning Malc decided to say arse several times out loud, in a variety of Tommy's different tones. That was it, a couple of minutes of imitating Tommy and being silly.

We visited the Colosseum that day and had a wonderful time in the city and returned to a gorgeous alfresco meal in their garden in true Italian style.

We'd had several drinks and were enjoying a great evening when:

"Arse"

John looked around at Tommy in the kitchen on his perch, who repeated the phrase in several variations to his favourite human – he was really pleased with himself; he had learned a new word.

John not so much. His head shot round to us as we stifled shocked giggles:

"Cheers guys, the vicar's due round tomorrow!" John forgave us almost immediately, seeing the funny side of it (of course Tommy couldn't unlearn this) also aided by the fact that he was the biggest practical joker we had ever met. Malc says he is a male Amanda, always looking for the next laugh.

The point of this Tommy story is that this little character kept appearing in my dreams, surprising because I hadn't really thought about him for several years. He would sit on my hospital bed at different times throughout that three-day period, even when I was dreaming other things. I can remember dreaming about Mum when me and Sal took her on holiday to a lighthouse in Devon following her recovery from her treatment for lung cancer. We were there for four days and had chosen the location because she wanted to be near to the sea – where nearer than a lighthouse. These were lovely memories to be having at this time, being with my Mum and Sister by the sea, enjoying the views and being watched over by my little parrot mate. I would even rouse from these dreams looking for him on the bed. I also remember our long weekend in Venice; Emma's eighteenth birthday present (instead of a party she said, we didn't argue, selfish?), looking up at the architecture and beautiful views, another special memory. Being photographed with Dan and Em in front of the Arc de Triomphe in Paris, in front of the traffic madness that surrounds that monument. Hello Tommy, you still here?

"Arse"

So, my dreams had laughter and happy times running through them, times spent with family and friends which was all very reassuring and comforting.

"Georgina, brrring, brrring"

Recent memories of our train journey to the Alps, stepping off the train into a foot of snow at the highest station in the Alps and breathing the clean, cool air whilst taking in the view in bright sunshine – absolutely gorgeous.

I thought about my darling Paul, my best friend from my early nursing days, who we were lucky enough to visit in Sydney several years ago and who took us on the Sydney art sculpture trail around the cliff tops of the bay starting off in Tamarama. One particular moment popped out, when Malc took a photo of me and Paul stood together inside a giant picture frame on the cliff edge, with the sea as our backdrop. This was an image that kept flashing up.

"Joshua, ciao, arse, cough, cough, cough" Alright mate?

Lots of positive thoughts and memories putting my life into perspective. Nothing (most surprising!) negative.

In the early hours of the morning on one particular night, I was quite unsettled and struggling with my breathing, when a nurse asked if there was anybody who would be awake who I could be put in contact with and I immediately thought of John and Helen who now lived on the Sunshine Coast in Australia (they had moved with John's flight engineer posting and we visited them on the same visit as we saw Paul in Sydney). The nurse got Helen's number up on my phone and we could see by the green dot that she was available, so the nurse called the number for me. Helen answered the phone, and it was a beautiful, bright sunny day in Australia - so surprising! There was Helen's gorgeous face looking back at me, goodness knows what she thought seeing this strained vision with tubes coming out all over the place. Luckily, she was a nurse and ex-paramedic – not phased in the slightest. It was difficult for me to speak with my breathing issues. She realised immediately what was going on and that I was in a bit of a pickle, so she took charge of the conversation and took me for a walk down to the surf. She was waiting to catch a boat and the sea breeze was blowing her hair about. I remember telling her about my visits from Tommy the Parrot, and we had a laugh about him and a short chat about why he might be visiting me. I didn't have enough energy or breath for swapping details about our families, but we'll catch up again soon. These few minutes spent with an old friend, in a virtual moment on the beach in Australia was incredible, a moment that took me out of my head and allowed me to calm down and was a great lift to my spirits. I don't remember the conversation ending, as I'd drifted off to sleep again.

I finally roused from the dream period after three days and logged back onto my phone and counted one hundred and eleven messages, various videos of support, just wonderful.

One of the messages stood out for unusual reasons. One of my nieces was born on 12/12/2012, so last December was her eighth birthday, and due to all the lockdown restrictions, I decided to send money and a parcel through the post, something I hate doing. I would much rather buy a gift.

And of course, the parcel never arrived. It was tracked and showed it was signed for, but even with various enquiries by my brother and his wife and exhaustive tracking by them it wasn't found. My brother did say he had a funny feeling it would turn up eventually, strangely positive considering he is very much a glass half empty type of character. Sure enough, amongst the messages there was a short video of Erin holding her belated birthday and Christmas cards and money that had arrived finally, only six weeks late!! My brother was so thrilled to send me this and again it gave me a lift.

I had messages and daily support from Sarah and Marcus, Steve and Jude and a virtual dog walk with Liz and her three labradors, videos of friends in the snow or cleaning out pet hutches, anything and everything to get my head out of hospital and into the real world:

Grandparents and Grandkids baking cakes;

Three lots of new kitchens being fitted or renovated, lots of regular updates;

Personal motivational video messages.

I received non-stop jokes and memes (hi Lorraine) and so much stuff to keep me going. It all played its part in moving me towards recovery and out of hospital. I cannot thank everybody enough; you all played a part in my return home.

Thank you!

CHAPTER TEN

My Spirituality

I have never considered myself as a spiritual person, I had always come from the medical side of things, life and ultimately death being a physical process. I have never seen anything in my life to convince me otherwise. I can remember the commonplace RE (Religious Education) classes at school and some Sunday school when I was young, but like many people I just got on with life and was certainly not a regular church goer – just christenings, weddings and funerals.

I have had friends through my life who have been "practicing" Christians, Catholics, and Jehovah Witnesses, who have regularly attended church or places of worship, and have played an active part in these communities including the service to their local communities.

I do consider that I am a spiritual person in that I do care for others and would never knowingly hurt anybody. I would like to think I always try to do the best I can from a morally correct point of view rather than a strictly religious point of view, although proper Christian values cannot be argued against and provide a framework we all try to follow.

Having been in hospital and surviving a near death experience, certainly opened my eyes to the real value of positive feelings from others towards me and this was brought home to me in my experience with the hospital chaplaincy and in particular Narinder. She offered me a source of positive friendship that I had not expected, purely through her belief that much can be offered to others in times of need through positive thought and prayer. Just seeing someone's face who genuinely believes this can be quite uplifting.

Narinder and I had several quite deep conversations about my understanding of my own spirituality. I hadn't really done this before, not taken to thinking in this way, and going through the same spoken gestures as most other people in difficult times such as I'm thinking of you, you are in our thoughts, sending you positive energy. I am in no way saying that these sentiments are lacking in any sincerity, just that in the situation I found myself in, genuine deep-felt belief in something beyond the here and now gave these sentiments and heart felt prayers from strangers much more empathy and in fact made me feel quite emotional. I was told of a couple of prayer groups that had been organised for me by friends and I found this quite moving. This came as a surprise to me after having explained to Narinder at out first meeting that I was not religious in the formal sense, and that I would feel a total fraud asking for God's help at this frightening time in my life. It would surely be pointless to suddenly request help from an entity that I had never really believed in. Narinder explained that this was not a problem as asking for Christians with strong beliefs to be held in their thoughts and prayers was not an issue with them and their positive love and support could only be good for all involved.

Since being at home for a few weeks, Narinder contacted me and asked if I could record a short video to put with several others being recorded by different faith leaders and others, to be shown at a Bath Abbey memorial service to commemorate those lost over the past Covid year in the local area, and as human and spiritual support for all of those affected. Malc became my cameraman, and this has been recorded and sent to be edited.

I did have a discussion with Narinder explaining that I had not had any sort of epiphany, I still felt that we live and then die with no journey beyond this, although our physical self and energy surely becomes part of everything again. But I did react much differently to the love and goodwill sent my way, it gave me a great sense of warmth and added into the positive energy that I needed to get through this illness.

So, I have to say honestly that I do not think this experience will see me as a churchgoer in the future, but on reflecting on my experiences with friends and colleagues and all of the staff and support workers over the past few weeks, and what their love and support has meant to me and how it has made me feel, I have perhaps seen a depth of spirituality within myself that I did not expect to find.

CHAPTER ELEVEN

Coming Home

It is a very strange feeling to come back home after an extended stay in hospital. You have the mixed emotions of excitement at getting back to your family and friends and home, but also the nervousness at losing the medical support and expertise that is just seconds away while you are under constant observation on the ward. So at first you feel a bit like a fish out of water, you've lost the institutional regime by which you get through the days in hospital, the regular observations, drug rounds, doctors rounds, drinks and meals etc. and have moved to your own timetable, a cup of tea when you want one, a snack here and a meal of what you want when you want (sort of, a bit based on Malc's culinary skills - or lack of). Let's just say he's a great heater upper, apart from his mean omelettes.

The great part of being back is just the familiar and much-loved surroundings and knick knacks (including Malc) that have been gathered over the years and which hold all of those special memories of people and places. It is definitely the case that these small bits and pieces of life can be taken for granted on a daily basis but coming back home after such an emotionally charged period away, these special mementos take on a new significance in bringing you back to your normal life, and you definitely appreciate each memory as if you were remembering them for the first time.

I did quite well when I first came home, I had already agreed with the hospital staff and Malc that I would sleep and live downstairs, to avoid over exertion on the stairs. I needed to take things really slowly and allow my body a chance to get better, especially my weakened left arm and leg. We were lucky that we had a really comfortable sofa bed we had bought a few years ago for when Mum and Alan came to stay (she had not been able to manage the stairs for some time) so Malc set this up together with the usual necessities – commode, bed table, hot water bottle etc.

Malc became my at home carer, amazing man that he is, caring for me 24/7 (he was on sick leave then furlough) and insisting that he sleep downstairs with me just in case, even though I wanted him to sleep upstairs as I would be very restless. He refused and stayed with me downstairs, he'd missed me as much as I had missed him while I'd been in hospital. This continued for a couple of weeks with me just pottering about – pottering from bed to commode to chair to bed etc. I pottered so much that Malc started calling me Harry. I also pottered to the fridge and snack drawer quite regularly. The combination of steroids, losing 1½ stone in hospital and only regaining my appetite in the last few days of my hospital stay, meant that I was now ready to feed my new appetite, so that's exactly what I did. A good friend did some "extras" shopping over and above our online big shop which included some really special chunky soups that were really easy to digest and got me through the first few day's home. On the third or fourth day back, Malc heated up some East End (Manzies) pie and mash - the stuff with the green liquor all over it – that we'd ordered online and had in the freezer. This tested Malc's heater upper skills to the max as he had pies in the oven, mash in the microwave and liquor heating up on the hob. It turned out great, and I stuffed myself over the next 90 minutes which was followed by my best and longest sleep in a couple of months – I think I succumbed to a pie and mash coma!!

I continued to be supported by the NHS whilst at home via the community re-enablement team, which looked at my physiotherapy and any necessary help aids for the house, to help me with bathing and showering etc. I needed to have a splint organised for my left hand to help stop my middle two fingers from curling into my palm and a shower stool. It was very strange to see my house equipped like those of my many patients over the years and I was really grateful for them. It did bring home that I was in for a longer road to recovery, and the medics are indicating that it will likely be 12 months from my hospital release before I will have reached my likely level of recovery.

Six days after arriving home, I woke up in the night with a severe pain in my left arm, again all of my health issues following the Covid illness were focussed on my left side. I didn't check any further until the morning when I asked Malc to check out the site of the pain, and I had developed a strange rash that was localised to the inside of my upper arm on the left side. The rash developed further down towards my elbow during the course of that morning, and was now raised, almost wrinkly and still quite sore. I at first thought it might be the start of shingles, although it didn't really look like a classic shingles rash, but I had no clue as to what else it would be. I decided to contact my GP, who took some notes and asked me to send some photos. The photos were forwarded to the Dermatology Dept. at the Bath RUH by the GP. We had to wait until next day for an answer from the RUH, following discussions between the dermatology and Covid Teams, who decided that due to a lack of other symptoms, the rash should be treated at home with a topical cream.

The rash lasted for about 6-7 days with regular application of the cream, and monitoring by my GP referring to photos supplied by me. The skin affected by the rash took on the appearance and feel of a wrinkled plastic crisp packet, a very peculiar effect. The wrinkled skin was eventually shed a bit like a scab, and I was left with new surface skin that felt just like a new-born baby's.

I got over this bump and continued to gently potter about the house and garden, and decided a couple of weeks in that I could try to do a small shop at the supermarket, with Malc of course. We got ready and drove out to the nearest supermarket, but about halfway around the store I realised I had made a mistake and started to feel totally drained of energy. We steadily finished the shopping and got back to the car, which seemed to take a huge effort and returned home. An hour or two after getting back in, I started to feel that something wasn't quite right. I began to feel very unwell with a heavy feeling in my chest the classic sign of heart palpitations, a fluttering feeling in my chest. I just knew that things weren't right with my heart rhythm and was very concerned – I thought I was over being very ill. I took some basic ob's from our home kit, namely BP (which had a very high reading of over 200) and oxygen level with the finger pulse oximeter. We contacted the GP and discussed what was happening and she asked Malc to call an ambulance via 999 and get an ECG, some oxygen therapy and a decision on what to do next. The paramedics decided immediately after running the ECG that my heart was in atrial fibrillation (the top chambers of the heart, the right and left atrium, were fluttering and not performing their normal regular pumping action) and that I would be taken into the RUH yet again for further treatment. I was really quite scared at this point, as I could feel that my heart was out of control with a pulse rate ranging from 44 to 144 beats per minute, without changing what I was doing physically.

On arrival at hospital, I was taken to the resuscitation area where my heart rate and rhythm was monitored, and I was started on a drug regime to try to get things back to normal. I was given a Covid test as a matter of course and was told at 6.00 next morning on the ward that I was positive.

I was alarmed as I had been discharged from the Covid ward over three weeks previously. This caused a lot of panic and concern on the ward until the consultant explained that I would present positive tests for several weeks post Covid, but was not openly infectious. Relief all round.

The physical characteristics of my heart and surrounding structures were thoroughly checked and I was delighted to be told that physically everything was sound, with no underlying issues, and that the symptoms were more than likely due to the effects of the Covid infection on my heart muscle, but that the heart rhythm should be controlled by medication. I would be followed up by the cardiac clinic outpatient's service. This has left me pretty nervous about what long term effects I may have been left with by the dreaded bug, but I know I am being looked after by a truly supportive health service.

I was discharged again.

Back home and I was under house arrest by Malc, the family and friends, back to pottering about and sleeping downstairs. No stairs, no going out, my recovery wings had been well and truly clipped. I continued with my left sided physiotherapy to improve the strength in my hand and leg with support from the community re-enablement team. I have been told that I will have a neurology clinic follow up in 16-18 weeks, which seems like forever away, but which is nothing in terms of recovery from neurological damage like mine, it is just a very slow process.

My initial confinement was enlightened a few times a week by visits from my darling little Grandson Jake, his smiling little face meaning the world. We had formed a family bubble with Emma, Luke and Jake, which I was now reaping the benefits of.

We continued to stay safe, only going out when absolutely necessary, just to avoid any possibility of contracting a new variant that would be passed on to our family.

I then received a phone call from the lovely Narinder, the hospital chaplain, totally out of the blue. She asked if I would like to take part in the Bath Abbey Commemorative Service in memory of all those who died in the pandemic. This would be a virtual service filmed in Bath Abbey, but also using footage supplied by invited guests who represented different aspects of the pandemic and those affected. I was asked to be one of the guest film segments, so Malc became cameraman, lighting man and director and off we went. Filming brought out both of our divas, but the clip was finished and sent to Narinder, and I was extremely proud that it was shown in the online service on the Bath Abbey website on 24th March 2021, the one year marking of the pandemic. It was a short four-minute summing up of my experiences and the support I had been given.

This video clip led on to a short interview with our local BBC TV news service, Points West and a 20-minute live interview on Radio Somerset the same morning. I was in demand.

So, that's my story guys and thank you for reading. I will continue to work hard to improve my physical condition, but I am under no illusion that I will quickly get back to one hundred percent. This is not me being negative, but acceptant of what may be, but I will give it my best shot.

I have to add that writing this story down has been a great way to release myself from the thoughts and memories of what has happened over the last couple of months of what has been a devastating year for all of us. I don't generally suffer with anxiety, but I have been through a lot in a short space of time that has taken a lot to deal with and could feel quite overwhelming. The process of writing my experiences down has allowed me to revisit what happened and to a great extent "put it away". I hope it will also be useful to my family and friends to more fully understand what happened and will be there for baby Jake – and if we are really lucky, further Grandchildren – so that they can fully understand what we were all going through at this time.

A percentage of the money raised by the sales of this book will be split between the Royal United Hospital for their wonderful care and Dorothy House for the great end of life care that they provide for patients in our communities.

CHAPTER TWELVE

The RUH and Dorothy House

We have lived in Radstock, Somerset since 1989 with Malc having transferred from Bedfordshire ambulance service to the Wiltshire service, based in Warminster. Radstock was just over the border and when we were house hunting prices were much more affordable and we had more choice. We love it here and it has always felt like home.

The Royal United Hospital (known locally by its initials, the RUH) has always been in the background of our lives, Malc delivering patients on a daily basis when at work and all of us using their services over the years for various ailments, routine appointments and emergencies – they have literally been lifesavers for us on several occasions – certainly, without our NHS which is far too often taken for granted, our family would look very different today, even without the terrible loss of Mum and Alan.'

A Bit Of History

The RUH is the major acute care hospital in Bath serving the surrounding communities and specialised referrals from further afield. The hospital has a 565-bed capacity on a site that covers 52 acres. For those non-farmers like me, that is very roughly 52 football pitches in area. It is currently operated by the RUH NHS Foundation Trust (I know, but there is no test at the end, so you don't need to memorise any of this).

Just a quickie on bed capacity, as we've picked up on lots of misinformation out there about empty wards and beds, meant to indicate that there is not a pandemic problem. The current bed state of a facility is based on the number of staff available to support the patients that are filling those beds. So, if the current number of beds in that hospital is 1000, but there are only enough staff to support 500 patients, then the bed capacity would be 500. There is little point in putting 500 patients in those empty beds with no staff to look after them. These figures are a gross exaggeration, but it more easily makes the point – those conspiracy guys showing a ward of empty beds to back up their nonsense really know how to manipulate the truth. We all know how hard the staff have worked and how stretched they are, so it is not surprising that hospitals are unable to cope with all of their beds being full all of the time.

Back to the history. The hospital takes its name from the union of two earlier major health care facilities in Bath, the Bath Casualty Hospital (f. 1788) and the Bath City Dispensary and Infirmary (f.1792). The Bath Casualty Hospital was set up to cater for the serious injuries that were being suffered by the workers involved in building the city. The dispensary and infirmary developed from The Bath Pauper Scheme (f. 1747), which was a charity scheme that provided medical treatment for anybody who was destitute in Bath.

The combined health care service opened a hospital in Bath in 1826, designed by John Pinch the Elder, in Bow Street, Bath and was called the Bath United Hospital. The Royal title was awarded by Queen Victoria in 1864, when a new wing, titled the Albert Wing after the recently deceased Prince Consort was opened. This building was later occupied by Bath College.

The hospital moved to its current location in Coombe Park in December 1932. This site had been used as a First World War hospital, the Bath War Hospital, opening in 1916, and was renamed the Bath Ministry of Pensions Hospital in 1919, which it remained until it closed in 1929. The original medieval manor house on the site was remodelled in the 1700's and later became an admin centre.

The site was also used by the Forbes Fraser Hospital and the Bath and Wessex Orthopaedic Hospital, both founded in 1924, and which both merged into the RUH that we know today in 1980.

The hospital also absorbed the Ear, Nose and Throat Hospital in 1959 and in 1973 the Bath Eye Infirmary.

More recently the state-of-the-art Dyson Centre for neonatal care was opened in 2011, to look after premature babies. Over half of the cost of the £6 million build was raised by the RUH's own charity, the Forever Friends Appeal. In 2015-16 some of the specialist services of the Royal National Hospital for Rheumatic Diseases, including endoscopy and children's services were transferred from its central Bath location. Subsequently the RUH NHS Foundation Trust took over all of rheumatic disease services and these have moved to a new dedicated building on the current site, with the transfer completed in the last couple of years.

The current RUH provides acute treatment and care for its catchment area of about ½ million people from Bath and the surrounding area in North East Somerset (BANES) and West Wiltshire.

The hospital provides clinical care for three commissioning clinical groups, BANES, Swindon and Wiltshire.

The hospital has many state of the art facilities, the most well known being the helicopter landing point that serves the accident and emergency unit.

Dorothy House Hospice

Dorothy House is a local hospice charity, with their main building based in Winsley, Wiltshire. The hospice was started 40 years ago in Bloomfield Road in Bath and was the vision of the Rev Prue Dufour MBE. Prue believed that no-one should die alone if this could be avoided, and thanks to her determination, Dorothy House has since provided end of life care to more than 45,000 patients, their families and carers. 40 years on, the staff are proud of their part in the radical transformation of the hospice service.

Dorothy House is currently the largest local independent end of life care provider. Our area of responsibility encompasses 550,000 people over 700 square miles of BANES and into Wiltshire and Somerset.

They provide a comprehensive range of services, including community nurse specialists, a ten bed inpatient unit, a Hospice at Home team and a range of therapies and bereavement support. It is a very special place indeed.

The new building at Winsley is ever growing and offers more and more services for inpatients and day patients, and hosts teams of specialists in palliative care. Inpatients usually have complex needs and require the most up to date practices to provide a peaceful, pain-free transition to end of life.

The grounds at Winsley are stunning, providing wonderful countryside views and a peaceful setting. There is plenty of wildlife about in the grounds, including deer and birds of prey, and we have our own resident duck – and I mean resident! She hatches her ducklings in the courtyard and then takes the ducklings to visit dad on the river, which requires a journey through patient room 2, under the bed out through the doors and down through the grounds to the river. This is a yearly experience, and the patients love it – the healing effect of animals. Although the job is physically tiring and can be very emotional, it is a lovely place to work and gives staff a great sense of pride to be a part of this service.

Of course, as a charity, Dorothy House – like all other charities including the Forever Friends Appeal – has been hit hard financially during the pandemic, which is why part of the proceeds from this book are going to these two charities.

Bath RUH

Dorothy House, Winsley

Printed in Great Britain
by Amazon

61942211R00030